D1314746

The Stars

The
Solar
System

Contents

©2016
Book Life
King's Lynn
Norfolk PE30 4LS

ISBN: 978-1-910512-85-2

Written by:
Gemma McMullen
Edited by:
Amy Allatson
Designed by:
Matt Rumbelow
Ian McMullen

A catalogue record for this book
is available from the British Library.

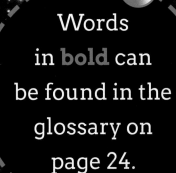

Words in **bold** can be found in the glossary on page 24.

The Solar System

The Sun

The Solar System is the Sun and all of the objects that **orbit**, or go around, it. Eight planets orbit the Sun, including our home, Earth.

4

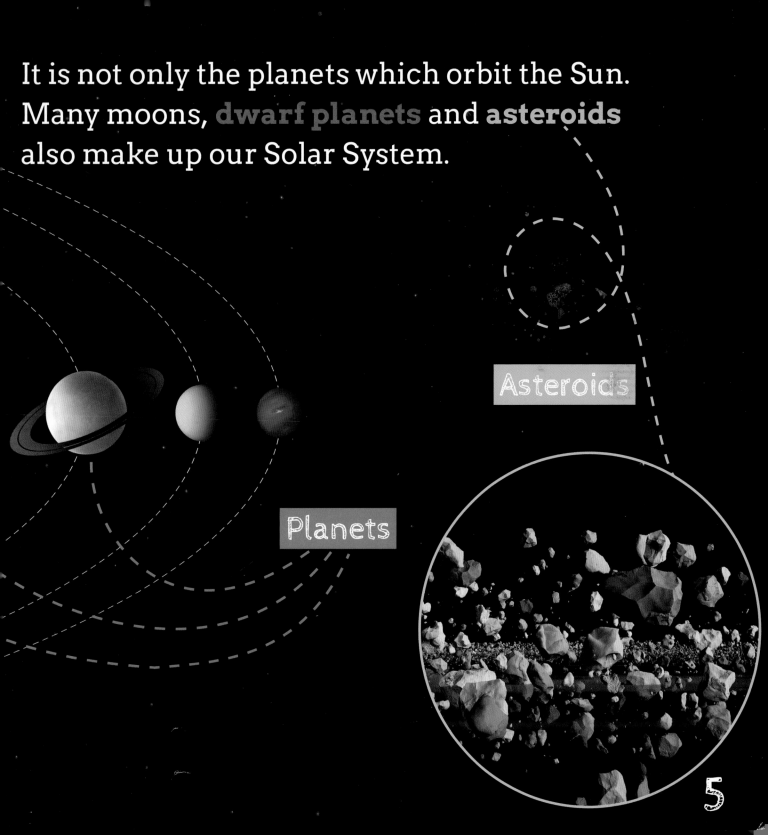

It is not only the planets which orbit the Sun.
Many moons, **dwarf planets** and **asteroids**
also make up our Solar System.

Asteroids

Planets

What are Stars?

Stars are giant balls of gas which are very hot and bright. Stars can be seen from our planet, Earth, during the night time. They look like tiny lights in the sky.

6

Stars are very far away from our planet which is why they look so small. They are actually very big.

Nearest Star

Earth

The Sun

The Sun is a star. It is the closest star to planet Earth which is why it seems larger than the rest.

The Sun

(Our closest star.)

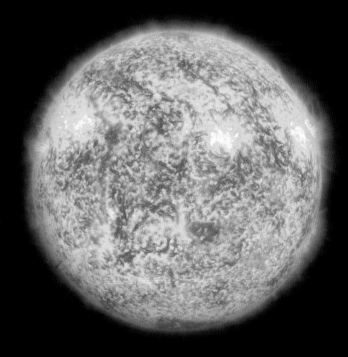

Alpha Centurai

(The second closest star.)

8

The sun lights and heats the planets in the Solar System. Without the sun, there would be no life on planet Earth.

Animals and plants need the sun so that they can grow.

Sizes and Colours

Not all stars are the same size and colour. Large stars are usually blue or red. Smaller stars are usually yellow.

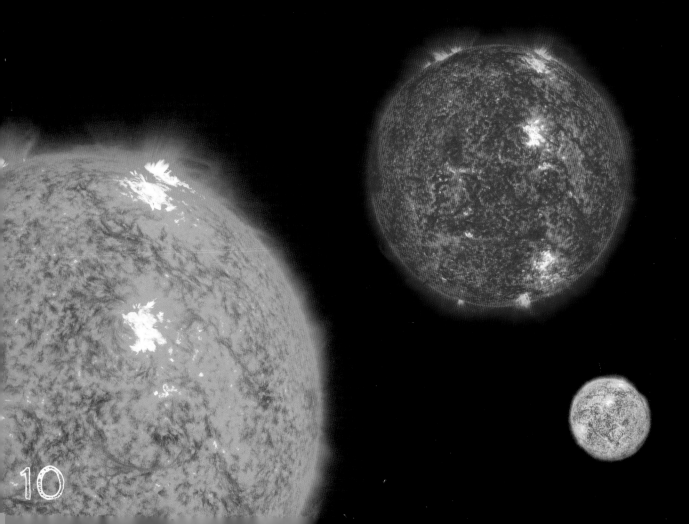

The Sun is a yellow star. Even though it is much bigger than our planet, it is still quite small for a star.

Blue
Supergiant

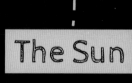

The Sun

There are
many stars
which are
larger than
the Sun.

Galaxies

A group of stars is called a galaxy. The Sun is part of a galaxy called the Milky Way. There are a lot of stars in the Milky Way.

The Milky Way is only one galaxy, there are lots of galaxies in space. Galaxies can be different shapes and sizes. Smaller galaxies have less stars.

Constellations

Constellations are groups of stars which look like a pattern or object when they are joined together. An example of a constellation is the plough.

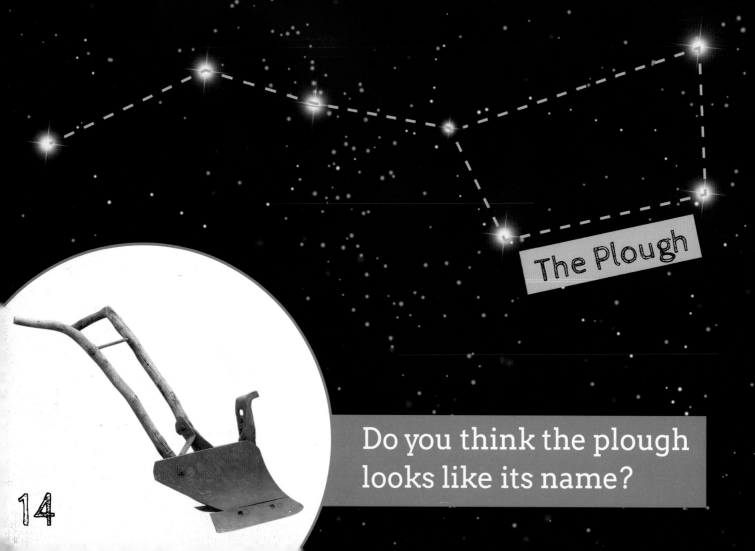

The Plough

Do you think the plough looks like its name?

The constellations help us to tell which stars are which. They are a bit like a map of the sky.

Star Map

Astronomy

An astronomer is a scientist who learns about and watches objects in space, including stars. We would not know as much as we do about stars without these scientists.

Telescopes help us to see stars even further away.

Exploding Star

We know that some stars get bigger and duller over many years. They slowly fade away. We also know that some big stars explode.

Stargazing

Many people enjoy looking at the stars in the sky and have done for thousands of years.

Many old myths and stories include stars.

All that is needed for stargazing is a dark, clear sky. It might be helpful to have a book about constellations to help you to spot them.

Shooting Stars

Sometimes it appears as though a star is shooting across the sky. A shooting star is not really a star, it is a hot piece of space rock called a meteor.

A shooting star is still very pretty to watch. Lots of shooting stars at once is called a meteor shower.

Super Star!

1 Bigger stars have shorter lives than smaller ones.

 Our sun is a yellow dwarf star..

3 The most common star is the red dwarf star.

4 Stars do not actually twinkle, it just seems like they do.

23

Glossary

Index

Photo Credits

Photocredits: Abbreviations: l-left, r-right, b-bottom, t-top, c-centre, m-middle. All images are courtesy of Shutterstock.com.
Front Cover — Triff. 1 – sNike. 2 - AstroStar. 4 - fluidworkshop. 5inset - Denis_A. 6, 6inset - Triff. 7 - Vadim Sadovski. 8l - Markus Gann. 8r - Triff. 9 - mironov. 9inset - spfotocz. 10, 11 - Triff. 12 - Alex Mit. 13 - clearviewstock. 14 - Santia. 14inset - Arogant. 15t - Baldas1950. 15b - Piotr Sikora. 16 - Triff. 17 - PandaWild. 18 - Zvereva Iana. 19 - Ollyy. 20, 21 - mmgemini. 22 - AstroStar. 22inset - Triff. 23t - manjik. 23b - Suzanne Tucker.